Nicholas Wright

VINCENT
IN BRIXTON

NICK HERN BOOKS
LONDON
www.nickhernbooks.co.uk

A Nick Hern Book

Vincent in Brixton was first published in Great Britain
as a paperback original in 2002 by Nick Hern Books Limited,
14 Larden Road, London W3 7ST

Vincent in Brixton copyright © by Nicholas Wright
Introduction copyright © by Nicholas Wright

Nicholas Wright has asserted his right to be identified
as author of this work

Front cover: 'Still Life with Pair of Boots', by Vincent Van Gogh,
reproduced with permission from the Baltimore Museum of Art.

Typeset by Country Setting, Kingsdown, Kent, CT14 8ES
Printed and bound in Great Britain by Bookmarque, Croydon, Surrey

A CIP catalogue record for this book is available from
the British Library

ISBN 185459 665 9

FOR DAVID

as always

'The Secrets at the Loyers . . . '

Artistic genius usually announces itself at an early age. Van
Gogh's was different. Nobody in the small country parish, where
his father was the pastor, spotted a painter in the making, least
of all himself. And when, at the age of sixteen, he took up a
junior post in The Hague with the international art-dealing firm
Goupil and Co., it wasn't a stepping-stone towards life as an
artist. No fewer than three of his uncles were art dealers and
young Vincent was simply being groomed for a middle-class
career in the family tradition.

At the age of twenty he was transferred to Goupil's London
gallery at the comfortable salary of £90 a year. Two years later,
at what seems to have been the instigation of his father, he was
transferred to the Paris branch. He came back to England after
a year to work as an unpaid schoolteacher, first in Ramsgate
and then in Isleworth, and, on December 20th 1876, he went
home to Holland for Christmas, never to return.

Years of preaching and drifting followed. It wasn't until the summer of 1880 that, in a long, passionate letter to his younger brother
Theo, he declared his intention to become an artist. 'The aim
becomes more definite, will stand out slowly and surely, as the
rough draft becomes a sketch, and the sketch becomes a picture –
little by little, by working seriously on it, by pondering over the
idea, vague at first, over the thought that was fleeting and passing,
till it gets fixed.' From now on, his letters are filled with descrip-
tions of his drawing and painting, along with urgent demands for
money and materials. His new life was to last for exactly ten
years: in 1890, at the age of thirty-seven, he shot himself.

Theo died six months later, leaving a baby son and a young
widow. In his role as an art-dealer for Goupil, he had sold not
a single one of Vincent's paintings. (Vincent's only sale came
about independently.) In her diary, Theo's widow now described
the responsibility she felt towards her fantastic inheritance: ' . . .
to show it, and to let it be appreciated as much as possible . . .

All the treasures that Theo and Vincent collected – to preserve them inviolate for the child.' For the rest of her long life she curated and guarded Vincent's paintings, skilfully steering them on to the international market.

Most of what we know about Vincent's life in England comes from her edition of his letters to Theo, and from her short memoir of him. Other clues survive in odd places: his name appears in the visitors' book of the British Museum's Department of Prints and Drawings, where he went to look at the Rembrandts, and there's a reference to a 'Mr. Vincent van Gof' in the minutes of Turnham Green Congregational Church. There are also the letters exchanged between Vincent's parents and siblings. These are vivid with the drama of a God-fearing family whose unstable son is at loose in a city of doubtful morality. When Vincent and his sister Anna abruptly left the Loyer household, their mother knew exactly who to blame. 'Since the summer he has been abnormal,' she wrote. 'The secrets at the Loyers did him no good'.

The Loyers' address – 87, Hackford Rd., SW9 – was unknown until 1971, when a London postman named Paul Chalcroft, who was also a keen amateur painter, took advantage of the long postal strike of that year to mount a search with the help of local records, census returns and (I like to think) his first-hand knowledge of the layout of local streets. Thanks to him the house now has a blue plaque and the identities of the schoolteacher-landlady, her young daughter and her other lodger are a matter of fact.

Vincent in Brixton is based on all these bits and pieces of evidence, but it goes much further than any biographer could do in interpreting them. (The most authoritative factual accounts can be found in Martin Bailey's book *Young Vincent* and his 1992 Exhibition Catalogue *Van Gogh in England*.) In speculating about what might have happened between the five inhabitants of this roomy, suburban house in the 1870s, I was encouraged by the partiality of family myth, by an intriguing six-month gap in Vincent's surviving letters and by the well-known tendency of young men writing home to be less than frank about their most formative experiences.

A significant part of the writing of the play was done as the result of a week-long workshop at the Royal National Theatre Studio. Thanks to Sue Higginson, who runs the Studio, to Richard Eyre, who directed the workshop, and to Tim Hatley, Emma Handy, Clare Higgins, Lee Ingleby, Lyndsey Marshal, Paul Ready, Maddy Grant and Eddie Keogh: the imaginations and energies of these old and new friends were crucial.

NW

Vincent in Brixton was first presented in the Cottesloe at the National Theatre on 24 April 2002. Press night was 1 May 2002. The cast was as follows:

URSULA LOYER	Clare Higgins
VINCENT VAN GOGH	Jochum ten Haaf
EUGENIE LOYER	Emily Blunt
SAM PLOWMAN	Paul Nicholls
ANNA VAN GOGH	Emma Handy

Director Richard Eyre
Designer Tim Hatley
Lighting Designer Peter Mumford
Music Dominic Muldowney
Sound Designer Neil Alexander

VINCENT IN BRIXTON

Characters

URSULA LOYER, *late forties*

VINCENT VAN GOGH, *twenty*

EUGENIE LOYER, *eighteen*

SAM PLOWMAN, *twenty-one*

ANNA VAN GOGH, *eighteen*

Time: 1873-1876

Place: The kitchen at 87 Hackford Road, London

ACT ONE

Winter. Sunday morning. A big wooden table, functional and unusual. A stove-cum-boiler. Pots of water boiling.

URSULA *shows* VINCENT *in. She's been showing him a room upstairs. She's dressed in black.* VINCENT *is twenty. He's smartly dressed in his Sunday suit, with a top hat and polished boots. Red hair.*

URSULA. Where are you staying at present?

VINCENT. In Greenwich. But the church . . .

URSULA *gets on with her cooking, picking up from where she left off before answering the door. At present she's peeling and trimming sprouts.*

. . . the church I attend is here in Brixton. Brixton Congregational Church. I like the service. It's sincere and plain. It is the kind of service I would attend at home. So it is worth the walk.

URSULA. The walk?

VINCENT. Oh, yes.

URSULA. Did you walk from Greenwich?

VINCENT. Yes.

URSULA. How long did it take you?

VINCENT. Two hours.

URSULA. Do you do a lot of walking, Mr. Vincent?

VINCENT. Yes.

URSULA. Do you walk to work?

VINCENT. Oh no!

He laughs.

It may be once or twice, at the end of the month, the state of my pocket means that I walk to work, but no, as a general rule I take the ha'penny steamboat to Waterloo Bridge and then I walk to Covent Garden. But on Sundays or on holidays, when I've no-one to talk to, then I walk as far as my legs will take me.

URSULA *puts salt and soda in a pot of boiling water and tips the sprouts in. Having done that, she starts chopping parsley. Meanwhile:*

URSULA. Don't you have any friends in London?

VINCENT. No. I don't know why. Perhaps I'm too forward in my feelings. Or I speak my mind too bluntly. But I cannot change my nature. You must know that, Mrs. Loyer. If it upsets you to have a plain, outspoken Dutchman in your house, then you must say so. I will bear you no ill-will. I will walk back to Greenwich with a good heart and proud of what God has made me. But I hope you will accept me as your lodger. I like the room which you have shown me. I like this part of London, it has a, how can I say, a Monday-morning-like sobriety about it which reminds me of Holland. What more can I add? I'm quiet. I'm an assiduous reader. I am a temperance man. I'd be a steady tenant for twelve months at least. Next year I hope to be transferred to Paris.

URSULA *starts assembling a pan-sized fish-cake: fish, mashed potatoes, parsley, white of egg, salt, pepper. In time she will brush it with egg and cover it in breadcrumbs. Meanwhile:*

URSULA. To Paris?

VINCENT. Yes.

URSULA. Do you speak French?

VINCENT. My French is . . . well, it's about as good as my English.

URSULA. *Vous parlez très bien Anglais. Avec un vocabulaire très bon. J'ai trouvé cet 'assiduous' tres impressionant.*

VINCENT. *Quant à vous, Madame, la façon dont vous parlez le Francais laisserai supposer que vous êtes au moins Francaise!*

URSULA. My husband was French. He was a teacher at the Grammar across the road.

VINCENT. I see.

There's a pause while URSULA *attends to the cooking.*

May I take the room?

URSULA. You haven't asked the rent.

VINCENT. No, I forgot.

URSULA. One moment.

She finishes what she was doing.

I charge twelve and sixpence a week, or eighteen shillings with breakfast and Sunday midday dinner. Is that agreeable?

VINCENT. Yes.

URSULA. Which do you want?

VINCENT. The breakfast, please, and the Sunday dinner.

URSULA. And how much notice must you give in your present arrangement?

VINCENT. One week.

URSULA. Then I shall see you on Sunday next.

VINCENT. Thank you. Thank you.

URSULA. You'll have a key, so you can come and go as it suits you. The dining-room's off the hall. Breakfast is served at seven.

VINCENT. Seven o'clock. I'll remember that.

URSULA. Your bath-night will be Wednesday. Fresh bedlinen is provided once a week. If you want any personal laundry done, Bridget will look after it for an additional one and sixpence. That's shirts twice a week, collars daily and all the rest of it.

VINCENT. Who is Bridget?

URSULA. Bridget's the maid. She isn't here today, she doesn't do Sundays. Your travelling-trunk, or anything large, we can put in the box-room. Do you play the piano?

VINCENT. No, I'm quiet in every way.

URSULA. I was only going to say that there's a piano in the schoolroom. Did I tell you about the school?

VINCENT. No?

URSULA. I run a small preparatory school for boys too young for the Grammar. They arrive very early, if both their parents are working. The door stands open and my daughter does the register. I hope they won't disturb you.

VINCENT. In fact I'm fond of children.

URSULA. Classes are held in the front room, ground floor, so there isn't a parlour. Use this kitchen whenever you like. Your food-cupboard will be there. I have to say, in the light of certain past experiences, that I don't encourage guests that I don't know about.

VINCENT. Of course.

URSULA. I'm sorry to point that out. I don't like rules and I hate imposing them on other people.

VINCENT. I see.

URSULA. This is an easy-going house. We're all progressive in our views. We're none of us churchgoers. I hope you're happy with that.

VINCENT. There are as many ways to God as there are people. So yes, I'm happy.

He stands, looks at his pocket-watch.

But I have missed my dinner.

URSULA. Why don't you eat with us?

VINCENT. Oh no, I couldn't impose.

URSULA. Please do.

VINCENT. Thank you.

Perhaps he sits. She drains a panful of potatoes.

URSULA. I can't be much in the way of company, I'm afraid. Would you like a book?

VINCENT. What books have you got?

URSULA. Dickens, of course. Have you read George Eliot?

VINCENT. No.

URSULA. You should. *The Mill on the Floss* would be the one to start with. There's a shelf on the lower landing. Help yourself.

VINCENT. May I not help you with the cooking?

URSULA. Have you cooked before?

VINCENT. No.

URSULA. You can do the potatoes.

Feels them to see if they're too hot.

Just take the skins off.

He picks up a knife.

No, not with a knife. Like this.

She shows him. EUGENIE *comes in. She's eighteen and very attractive.*

EUGENIE. We're short of a serving-spoon.

URSULA. I've got it. Darling, this is Mr. Vincent. Mr. Vincent, this is my daughter Eugenie.

EUGENIE. Hello again.

VINCENT. I'm sorry, I can't shake hands.

EUGENIE. Don't bother. Have you come about the room?

VINCENT. I have. I'm happy to say that . . .

URSULA. Mr. Vincent's moving in next weekend. And he's staying for dinner.

EUGENIE. I'll lay him a place.

She goes. URSULA *finishes assembling the fish-cake.*

URSULA. Have you met my daughter before?

VINCENT. Not met, exactly. And I don't know why it slipped my mind to tell you. I was coming from church this morning, and my eye was caught by the sight of a young man outside on a piano stool. He was sitting in the winter sunlight drawing this house. I stopped to talk. Then your daughter came out and brought him a cup of tea. I thought it must be a friendly house where people drink their tea on the pavement. Then I saw the sign in your window, 'Room to Let'.

URSULA. That was Mr. Plowman you were talking to. He's my other lodger.

VINCENT. Yes, he told me.

URSULA. Did you form an opinion of his drawing?

VINCENT. No.

URSULA. You must have seen it.

VINCENT. Well, you know, I've met a lot of artists in my line of work, and the one thing they agree about is that they don't like people looking at what they're doing and passing comments.

URSULA. Mr. Plowman's a remarkable man. He was a parish boy. Do you know what that means?

VINCENT. No.

URSULA. An orphan.

VINCENT. Ah.

URSULA. He's had to struggle. Do you see that border around the room?

VINCENT *looks at it.*

VINCENT. Oh yes.

URSULA. He painted that. It's cherry-blossom. He copied it from a Japanese manuscript.

VINCENT. I see.

URSULA. Just because a room's a kitchen, it doesn't have to be ugly. Do you like the table?

VINCENT. Yes it's . . . ah . . . it's unusual.

URSULA. My husband found it in a barn in Sussex. The farmer brought it up on his cart. I scrub it with scouring-powder. That's why the grain stands out. I think that things in the house are much more beautiful when they're plain and simple.

She puts the fish-cake on to fry. SAM *comes in with his portfolio and pencils. He's twenty-one and a Londoner.*

There you are. I looked for you out the window and you'd disappeared.

SAM. It clouded over. I'll do that.

URSULA. Will you, Sammy? That would be nice.

SAM *takes over the fish-cake.*

Dinner will be at one, Mr. Vincent. You'll have to look after yourself till then.

SAM. I'll talk to him. I'll talk to anyone.

She goes. SAM *goes to his cupboard, and divides his time between pouring a couple of beers and keeping an eye on the fish-cake.* VINCENT *carries on peeling potatoes.* SAM *takes this in.*

You're settling in.

VINCENT. I am. I feel at home already.

SAM. Fancy a beer?

VINCENT. Oh no, I . . . maybe just one.

SAM. There's three brown ales and a bottle of Guinness. I recommend the Guinness.

VINCENT. Whatever you like. Tell me, Mr. Plowman, are you . . . ?

SAM. Call me Sam.

VINCENT. I will. And you must call me Vincent. Tell me, Sam, is it the fact that . . . ?

SAM. Hang on, hang on. You said your name was *Mr.* Vincent.

VINCENT. I did. But now you must call me Vincent plain and simple.

SAM. You mean your name is Vincent Vincent?

VINCENT. No. Only my Christian name is Vincent. But I use it as my family name, because there's almost nobody in this country who can pronounce my real one. Though it isn't in fact a difficult name. If you think of the Scottish word for a stretch of water, 'loch', and then you roll it together and first say 'fun', like 'jolly good fun'. 'Van Gogh'. Don't try it please.

He takes the Guinness.

Your health.

SAM. Cheers.

VINCENT. And now I can't any longer stem my curiosity. You were drawing outside. And then that very attractive border. Are you an artist?

SAM. Yes.

VINCENT. What medium do you work in?

SAM. Paint.

VINCENT. What do you paint?

SAM. Walls and ceilings.

VINCENT. Sorry, I don't . . .

SAM. I'm a painter and decorator. I work on a building team. I do friezes, dadoes, borders and a spot of ornamental plasterwork.

VINCENT. So you're a manual workman?

He laughs good-naturedly.

I thought that . . . No, forget it.

SAM. Can we get this straight?

VINCENT. Yes.

SAM. When the first caveman sat in his cave, he thought about what he'd seen that day, and the next thing he knew he was standing at the wall, with a piece of ochre in his hand, painting an antelope with an arrow stuck through its nut. He didn't sign it, it wasn't for sale and he didn't think it made him anyone special. You look at it now and it's a masterpiece.

VINCENT. I see. But . . .

SAM. I'll give you another example. There's a cutter, a carver in stone, and it's the middle ages, and he's carving rows of angels in a cathedral roof. Have you got cathedrals where you come from?

VINCENT. Not that kind. Go on.

SAM. Well, after months and months he thinks, oh blow these angels, just for once I'll carve the pop-eyed, knobbly face of my sod of a foreman. We look at it now, and there's this wonderful thing, this marvel, it's the warmest, loveliest thing in the whole cathedral.

VINCENT. So what are you saying?

SAM. I'm saying that art is the rightful property of the working man.

VINCENT. I'll take your word for it. I myself have no artistic talent. But I spend my life in the spiritual company of those who do. I am an art dealer.

SAM. You didn't tell me that.

VINCENT. Well, it's nothing to brag about. My card. No, it is in my weekday suit. I work as a junior sales-assistant for the London branch of Goupil and Company. They're an international firm of art dealers, based in The Hague. I've been transferred to the London branch in the hope that I will gain experience.

SAM. And have you?

VINCENT. Not of the kind I wanted.

EUGENIE *comes in with a carving-knife and fork in a box, which she leaves on the table.*

EUGENIE. Where've you been, Mr. Plowman?

SAM. I went for a stroll.

EUGENIE. You went to the pub, you liar. I believe you've succumbed to a girl down there.

SAM. What I succumbed to, Miss Loyer, was the siren song of Pilk's Brown Ale. I'm about to do it again what's more. (*To* VINCENT.) You on for that?

VINCENT. No, thank you.

SAM *gets another beer.* VINCENT *watches* EUGENIE *as she goes out.*

Tell me, Sam . . . Have you a girl?

SAM. A what?

VINCENT. A girl. Have you got one?

SAM. Can you keep a secret?

VINCENT. No.

SAM. Not ever?

VINCENT. No.

SAM. I'll tell you anyway. I'm the wolf that walks alone.

VINCENT. I see. But why no girl? A good-looking man like you?

SAM. Well, doing a job like mine, I can't afford to take girls out. Besides, at the end of a hard day's work I haven't got the energy.

VINCENT. I've got so much energy, I think I'll burst. I sit at my desk, and try to fill my head with noble thoughts. Then I see some detail in a nude by Ingres and . . .

He gestures in despair.

Perhaps if I found some physical outlet such as you have. That might help. There's a man who breaks the ice in the park for his morning swim. I've seen him often. But the children laugh and point at him, I wouldn't like that. No, the only thing that would stop me thinking about girls all day is a girl.

SAM. Well there's a lot of nice girls in London.

VINCENT. I know. I see them every place I go. There were days last summer when there seemed to be nobody else but girls. But I can't walk up to a girl I've never met and start up a conversation.

SAM. Why not?

VINCENT. Because I wasn't brought up like that. When I left home, my father gave me three pieces of advice. Write to your mother. Don't take up smoking. Never talk to strange girls.

SAM. What about girls at work?

VINCENT. Oh well, it's funny that you should say that, because there is in fact a girl who works in the dispatch department. Miss Beddoes. Big shoulders, broad strong face, you'd almost think she was a Dutch girl. She's, how can I say, she's oh, she's . . .

Gestures.

. . . well, to cut a long story short, I thought I'd ask her to the show at the Empire. I walked to the dispatch department thinking, this is absurd, I don't like music-halls, I go to galleries and museums, she knows that. She'll know that what I'm wanting to say is, 'Miss Beddoes, I want to unbutton your blouse.' Or something worse. I opened her door, and what did I ask her? 'Miss Beddoes, why were you five minutes late for work this morning?' So that was a fine success. I went back to my desk and wanted to stick my paper-knife into me, that is how bad I felt.

SAM. You know your problem?

VINCENT. Yes. No.

SAM. Premeditation.

VINCENT *doesn't know this word.*

Thinking ahead.

VINCENT. You're right.

SAM. If there's something you want in life, you've got to grab it.

VINCENT. Then I'd have grabbed Miss Beddoes.

SAM. She might not mind. She might have been sitting on toast for weeks. Why don't you try it tomorrow?

VINCENT. No, I've missed my chance.

Pause.

So you are alone. And I am alone. And Mrs. Loyer is also, of course, alone. That leaves only her daughter. Though Miss Loyer I'm sure has many admirers.

SAM. Oh no.

VINCENT. Why not?

SAM. Because she's wedded to her vocation.

VINCENT. What do you mean?

SAM. She helps her mother run the school. Her mother can't do without her. It's as simple as that.

VINCENT. That's nonsense. The woman I saw could run a factory, let alone a school for little children.

SAM. You're seeing her on a good day.

VINCENT. Am I?

SAM. Oh, a *very* good day.

SAM *checks the fish-cake, shifts it in the pan.* VINCENT *waits.*

Did you notice anything odd about the way she was dressed?

VINCENT. She was dressed in black.

SAM. Did that not strike you as unusual?

VINCENT. No. In Holland it's quite normal for a widow to dress in black.

SAM. Well not in England. Not when the gentleman in question died fifteen years ago. Unless you're eighty or the Queen or something. Shall I give you a tip?

VINCENT. Please do.

SAM. Nothing in this house is what it seems.

VINCENT. Well I must think about that.

EUGENIE *comes in with serving-dishes. She drains the sprouts and puts them in a dish. Puts the potatoes in a dish. Then, at the range, she puts butter on to melt, prior to making a roux for parsley sauce.* SAM *takes off the fish-cake. Meanwhile:*

EUGENIE. Have you looked around the area, Mr. Vincent?

VINCENT. No.

EUGENIE. There's a very nice patch of meadow around the back. You'd just have time if you wanted to see it.

SAM. He's not going anywhere.

He opens the Guinness, perhaps splits it with VINCENT.

EUGENIE. Did you finish your drawing, Mr. Plowman?

SAM. Mm hm.

EUGENIE. Can't we see it?

SAM. Look at it later.

EUGENIE. Why not now?

VINCENT. I think that Sam is embarrassed to show it in my presence.

EUGENIE. Why should that put him off?

SAM. My fellow-lodger earns his living in the dubious trade of turning paintings into commodities.

VINCENT. In fact I don't sell paintings. In Holland, I did. I was salesman of the year in Holland. Here in London, we sell etchings, lithographs and photogravure reproductions. By post. It isn't the kind of work I'm used to. But I mustn't complain. I can visit the public galleries, I can train my eye.

SAM. What do you like? When you go to the galleries?

VINCENT. Well, you know, it takes a while to find the knack of liking English painting and I haven't yet done so.

SAM. There must be someone.

He passes EUGENIE *the milk. She pours it into the pan, then moves away, leaving him with the spoon. He stirs the sauce.* EUGENIE *finishes and garnishes the fish-cake, then washes her hands. Meanwhile:*

VINCENT. There was a painting at the Summer Exhibition. 'Devonshire House'. Quite a romantic work. A woman and her daughter are climbing the stairs of a banqueting hall. They're in their ball-gowns, and the daughter is looking ahead, like this, with a look on her face, and it's impossible not to assume she's seen some gentleman who's of interest to her.

He looks meaningfully at EUGENIE.

Perhaps Miss Loyer would like to see it.

SAM. I know that picture.

EUGENIE (*ironic*). Why don't you tell us about it, Mr. Plowman?

SAM. Not if you're going to be sarky.

EUGENIE. Mr. Plowman thinks pictures like that are an insult to the working population.

SAM. They are.

VINCENT *laughs.*

VINCENT. Well the working population doesn't agree with you, Sam, because we sell a reproduction of 'Devonshire House' for two and sixpence. It's one of our most popular lines.

SAM. I bet it is. I saw it last week, in the house of a man in my team, a casual. In his stinking bedsit, with a hole in the carpet. There on the wall was a marble staircase and two rich women in ballroom gowns. I thought it was obscene.

VINCENT. Aren't you being a little bit heavy-handed over something that isn't important?

SAM. It is important. That man had been robbed of his sense of beauty. Beauty was under his nose, if he only could see it. In his builder's hands and his broken-down boots. I'll tell you a beautiful picture. Same exhibition, next-door room. It's a night scene. There's a half-dead lamp over a gateway and people in rags, all waiting for their bed for the night. It's cold, they're freezing. You can't see hardly anyone's faces except for a man with a stick and a parcel. He's blind, he's given a scrap of paper to a copper and the copper's reading it out to him. It's a picture of hell, except it's real. People say, oh nobody wants to know about gloomy things, well that's all rubbish. There was such a crowd around that picture they had to put up a railing. It's nice to know not everyone's caught the same brain-rot that afflicts your customers.

EUGENIE (*with his portfolio*). Am I looking at this?

SAM. Yes if you like. (*To* VINCENT.) Hang on to this and push it about a bit.

VINCENT *takes the spoon and stirs the parsley sauce, drawn all the time to events at the table. Some danger of the milk boiling over.* SAM *opens his portfolio to show his drawing.* EUGENIE *looks at it.*

EUGENIE. It's very delicate. It's full of tiny details, like a puzzle.

SAM. Will you accept it? In return for that kind remark?

EUGENIE. Thank you.

She looks at it. VINCENT *breaks the silence, speaking loudly.*

VINCENT. I also draw. Some months ago I did a sketch of my room to send to my parents. They thought it was good. My mother especially.

No response.

Since then, my work at the gallery has been too demanding for such pastimes.

EUGENIE. It can go in the hall.

VINCENT. Also, of course, the urge to draw is curbed by modesty. One of my uncles has a fine collection. He's a director of Goupil and Company. I've seen at his house, originals by Frans Hals and Rembrandt. With such magnificence in the world, what is the point of adding one's own pathetic scribblings?

SAM *has poured the parsley sauce onto the fish-cake.*

SAM. I'll take this through.

He goes out with the fish-cake.

EUGENIE. That was very rude of you, Mr. Vincent.

VINCENT. Look at this drawing. Look at it. What do you see? A house. What kind of a house? Can you tell? I can't. Look at that line. What kind of artist uses a ruler? I'll show you. Where is a pencil?

He grabs one of SAM*'s and is about to correct the drawing.*

EUGENIE. Leave it alone! How dare you?

VINCENT *stops.*

That's a disgraceful thing to do.

VINCENT. I'm sorry.

EUGENIE. You should respect other people's property.

VINCENT. I will. Take the pencil. No, I'll break it.

EUGENIE. Give it to me.

VINCENT. I'll do you a drawing. It will be better, much better than that. I'll draw the meadow outside. I'll draw *you*.

EUGENIE. Will you take this please?

She gives him a serving-dish. URSULA *comes in.*

URSULA. I forgot the sprouts.

EUGENIE. I've done them.

She leaves with the drawing. VINCENT *stands holding the serving dish, upset.*

URSULA. Are you all right?

VINCENT. I made a fool of myself. I was put in a rage.

URSULA *takes the meat out of the oven: it's a leg of mutton, like the one in 'Alice Through the Looking-Glass', garnished with roast potatoes. Meanwhile:*

URSULA. So I gathered. If you disagree with Mr. Plowman, you should debate it properly. Can you help me with this, please?

He helps her transfer the leg of mutton to a serving-dish. He's clumsy and the job takes time, during which the scene continues. URSULA *starts making gravy in the roasting-pan.*

He's hoping to go to an art college, did he tell you?

VINCENT. No.

URSULA. He'll need a scholarship.

VINCENT. Of course.

URSULA. What I don't know, and neither does he, is what the people who decide these matters look for in a potential student. I'm sure that any advice you care to offer him would be more than welcome.

VINCENT. That's not possible, Mrs. Loyer. I insulted him. If he were Michelangelo, I couldn't have borne to hear your daughter praise his drawing.

URSULA. Why?

VINCENT. Because I love her. I've loved her from the moment
I saw her come out of the house this morning. She crossed the
road with a cup of tea in her hand, not spilling a drop. I tipped
my hat. And then I saw your sign, like a message from fate.
That was the only reason I rang your doorbell. Never in all
my life have I followed a girl. I know you need her for your
school. I respect that. But I . . .

URSULA. Will you stop this please?

VINCENT. Maybe on Sunday next, we can discuss it?

URSULA. Certainly not. We have to reconsider the whole
arrangement. I think you shouldn't move in. I think you
should stay in Greenwich.

*She continues with the gravy, stirring and reducing it.
Ketchup, salt and herbs are needed. After a few moments:*

I can't expose my daughter to the kind of overture which
I happen to know she wouldn't welcome.

VINCENT. Can I come for a month?

URSULA. What would be the point of that?

VINCENT. There's company here. There's you, with whom
I share so many interests. There's even an artist in the house.

He continues with passion. URSULA *slowly stops stirring,
turns to look at him.*

A fine good-hearted fellow who I'd be happy to help. Though
it will hurt me. And attack me where I'm weakest. But I can't
go back to my life as it was before. What can I say, what vow
can I give you? Tell me.

After a moment:

URSULA. I'm probably making a great mistake. But I'll let you
stay for a couple of weeks. Until you find some other
accommodation.

VINCENT. Thank you.

URSULA. You're not to trouble my daughter. You are not to confide in Sam. You will do nothing, nothing at all, which might reveal your inclination.

VINCENT. I promise.

EUGENIE *comes in.*

URSULA. There you are. Will you finish the gravy?

She and VINCENT *go out with the leg of mutton and the vegetables.* EUGENIE *stirs the gravy in the pan.* SAM *comes in, gets out the carving-knife and fork, sharpens the knife on a whetstone.*

EUGENIE. That's a very stormy fellow, Mr. Plowman.

SAM. He's just foreign, Miss Loyer.

Stops sharpening. Looks at the knife.

That's better.

He gets up, moves over to her.

How are we doing?

He looks at the gravy.

EUGENIE. See for yourself.

SAM. Smells good.

They kiss, not for the first time.

End of Act One.

ACT TWO

Spring. Sunday afternoon. It's sunny outside. There's an old book on the table and a pile of exercise books.

URSULA *comes in. She's been walking. She's tired and very upset. Maybe she fills the kettle, but she doesn't put it on. Sits.*

VINCENT *appears at the garden door, dishevelled and sweaty. After a few moments:*

VINCENT. Good afternoon, Mrs. Loyer!

URSULA *sees him.*

URSULA. I thought you were out. You gave me quite a turn. What on earth are you doing?

VINCENT. I'm digging the garden.

She sees his muddy boots and trousers, then looks past him into the garden.

URSULA. I see.

VINCENT. Do you want me to stop?

URSULA. No, no, it's very kind of you to bother. I wasn't expecting it, that's all.

She puts the kettle on the stove. He moves into the room.

No, don't come in with your boots like that. Do you want some tea?

VINCENT. I'll have a beer.

URSULA. I doubt there is any.

VINCENT. I bought some.

URSULA *opens his cupboard, which contains bottles she hadn't expected.*

URSULA. So you did.

She takes out a bottle.

I thought you were a temperance man.

VINCENT. I was denying myself. Now I do as I please. You don't object?

URSULA. Oh no.

She opens the bottle.

I'll get you a glass. Will you bring it back in?

VINCENT. May I not stay and drink my beer with you?

URSULA. Yes, if you like. I have some books to correct.

She opens an exercise-book, starts marking it. He takes his boots off, comes in and washes his hands. That done, he sits and fills and lights a pipe. Meanwhile:

VINCENT. This is a special occasion.

URSULA. Why?

VINCENT. We have the house to ourselves. Your daughter has gone to stay in Broadstairs. Sam is on his sketching holiday in Kent.

URSULA. I see what you mean.

VINCENT. Though when I looked it up in your Pears Cyclopaedia, it said that Broadstairs is also in Kent.

URSULA. Why did you look it up?

VINCENT. Oh, not because your daughter has gone there, I assure you. Not at all.

Pause.

Or, not in the first place. And I've promised you not to talk about that. You see, at Goupil and Company we sell a copy of a drawing which was done in Broadstairs. It's the chair in which Charles Dickens wrote *David Copperfield* and *Dombey and Son* I believe, and *The Old Curiosity Shop.* Have you seen it?

URSULA. No I don't think so.

VINCENT. It's called 'The Empty Chair'. That is all you notice
in the picture. Just the chair. But when you look, you see the
character of the man who sat in it. What do you think of that?
I must tell Sam about it. He could use it. I wish I had gone
with him on his sketching holiday. We could have had good
long talks. Politics, economics, all those topics on which I am
such a dunce. But he was right to refuse me. Art is a lonely
road. Do you think that Sam will get that scholarship?

URSULA. Do you?

VINCENT. Who can say? His drawing is better now. I think my
advice has helped him, now that I've learned to be not so
tactless. But he must build up his portfolio.

URSULA (*dry*). Yes, exactly.

VINCENT. Are you sad today?

URSULA. No, not especially.

VINCENT. That means you are. You see! I'm learning
diplomatic English. What is wrong?

URSULA. It's nothing. I don't like Sundays at the best of times.
And it's hot and my shoes are too tight and the little boys
will be clattering down the hall tomorrow. Really that's all.

*He nods, picks up the old book on the table and reads. Marks
a page with a matchstick or a bit of paper. There are already
markers in it. She goes on marking. After a while:*

VINCENT. The weather is beautiful now. I think that Spring
comes earlier here than it does in Holland. All last week,
when I walked to work, there were apple trees in blossom,
lilacs, hawthorns, chestnut trees. If you love nature, you can
find beauty anywhere, even in a city. This morning I woke at
six. I went for a walk on the common. The sky was blue and
a lark was singing. I ran to the church as though I was carried
by wings, and I sang so joyfully that all the people around
me turned and stared. When I came back, the house was
empty. I smoked. I read. But then I was troubled with
thoughts I would rather not have, so I went outside and took

up my spade and smote the earth with all my strength and the thoughts took flight.

He shows her the seed-packets. They look at them together.

These are what I will sow when I've raked it flat. Poppies. But I cannot guarantee they will be as bright and red as they are on the packet. Lupins. They'll go by the shed. Sweet peas.

Their heads are close.

Does my smoke annoy you?

URSULA. Oh no. In fact the smell has very pleasant associations for me.

VINCENT. Did your husband smoke?

URSULA. My father did. He was the captain of a ship. We often wouldn't see him for months on end. Then I'd come home from school, and there he'd be. Or I'd wake in the morning, and a marvellous scent would be winding its way up the stairs. That was his Dutch tobacco, very like yours.

VINCENT. My pipe, for me, is the best cure for unhappy feelings. The next is sunlight. And the last is work, hard physical work like now.

She gives him back the seed-packets.

URSULA. Thank you.

She opens an exercise book.

VINCENT. Where were you?

URSULA. When?

VINCENT. This afternoon, when the house was empty.

URSULA. I'd taken Eugenie to the station.

VINCENT. Of course!

Pause.

But you were gone all afternoon.

URSULA. We had to wait. It seems she'd looked up the train in the weekday column, rather than the Sunday one.

VINCENT. Let's hope your sister has not made the same mistake.

URSULA. What?

VINCENT. She said your sister would be meeting her off the train in Broadstairs.

URSULA. I'm sure she will.

VINCENT. But if she . . .

URSULA. What are you reading?

VINCENT. This? It's by Jules Michelet. *L'Amour*. It is a mostly philosophical work, despite the title. In fact I found it among your books. It has your husband's name inside.

URSULA. Yes, it was his. Let me see it.

He gives it to her. She looks at the flyleaf, looks inside the book.

Why have you marked the pages?

VINCENT. So I can write about them to my brother.

URSULA *opens and reads:*

URSULA. '*Un jeune homme voit dans Paris une belle demoiselle de traits réguliers. Il est épris.*'

VINCENT. 'Epris', I think, is a very nice word to say 'in love'.

She reads on, translating as she goes:

URSULA. 'He marries her, and then he wants to visit the place where she was born, the town of Arles. Once in Arles, he finds her everywhere, this woman he thought unique. He sees a hundred, a thousand girls, all just as lovely. It was the spirit of Arles which had seduced him.' How old's your brother?

VINCENT. Seventeen. I thought he would like to know of a place where there are thousands of beautiful girls.

URSULA. Is he at school?

VINCENT. He's with Goupil. He isn't like me. He has more . . .
aim in life. Then there's my baby brother, and three sisters,
Anna, Lies and Wilhelmien. But it is Anna that I must tell
you about.

URSULA. Why?

VINCENT. In the summer, I shall go home to Holland for a
fortnight. When I return, I will be bringing my sister Anna
here to London. She hopes to find a job as a governess with
an English family. She's only eighteen and she's never left
home. So it would set my parents' minds at ease if she could
live in this house.

URSULA. Do you mean, in . . . ?

VINCENT. Yes, in my room. And I'll move out.

She gives him back the book.

URSULA. I think that would be an excellent idea.

VINCENT. You do?

URSULA. I do. I'm glad you suggested it. I really do think it
will be better for everyone.

VINCENT. Thank you! Thank you! I know you will like her.
She is a modest, pious girl. With a passion for housekeeping.
You'll see her cleaning the windows, scouring the saucepans,
scrubbing the doorstep. And I shall move into the box-room.

URSULA. What?

VINCENT. For most people, of course, that room would be too
small. But I have nothing. I have a suitcase.

URSULA. You'll stay here, do you mean?

VINCENT. She's my sister. How can I leave her alone in
London?

URSULA. Mr. Vincent . . .

VINCENT. What?

URSULA. Are you quite sure you wouldn't like some tea?

VINCENT. I'll have a beer.

URSULA. I'll get it.

She gives him a beer, makes tea for herself.

I knew there was something odd going on when I found you digging up the garden.

VINCENT. In Holland I work in the garden all the time . . .

URSULA. I'm sure you do.

VINCENT. I sow not only flowers but turnips, potatoes, cabbage . . .

URSULA. Listen to me. I realised then that you didn't intend to leave. And now that you talk of staying on into the summer . . .

VINCENT. Well?

Pause.

URSULA. Mr. Vincent, do you still love my daughter?

VINCENT. Yes.

URSULA. Are you quite certain of that?

VINCENT. Of course.

URSULA. Then I think you should move. Move out. As we agreed.

VINCENT. But that was months ago.

URSULA. Exactly.

VINCENT. No. I can't accept this. If you want to throw me out, you should have done it the day I arrived.

URSULA. You're right. I should have.

VINCENT. Why didn't you?

URSULA. I don't know.

VINCENT. I've kept my promise.

URSULA. You have.

VINCENT. I've said nothing to her, nothing!

URSULA. No I know you haven't.

VINCENT. It isn't a nice position, being the rejected lover who hasn't even had the chance to be rejected.

URSULA. That's why I think we ought to end the situation.

VINCENT. But you've never once said that. Never till now. Why's that?

Pause.

You see? You haven't an answer.

URSULA. In fact I do.

VINCENT. What is it?

URSULA. It's that I cannot believe you're anything like as much in love as you imagine.

VINCENT. Why not?

URSULA. Because . . . well, if your feelings are as strong as you said they were, I don't see how you could suppress them. It isn't your nature.

VINCENT. So you know my nature?

URSULA. I think so.

VINCENT. You've never said *that* before.

URSULA. I haven't needed to.

She pours tea for herself.

VINCENT. So . . . if I wasn't . . . as I am . . .

He laughs.

It's strange I even consider it. If your daughter was just your daughter to me . . . then I could stay.

URSULA. But why would you want to?

VINCENT. That's what I ask myself.

URSULA. It's not my cooking.

VINCENT. In fact I'm getting to like your cooking. And there's you. We both speak French. We read the same books. *Jude the Obscure. Felix Holt, the Radical.* What would I know about the lives of working people, if it wasn't for you?

URSULA. And Sam.

VINCENT. And Sam. Oh well, I'll never be Sam. But isn't there something deeper than that between us?

URSULA. What?

VINCENT. Don't you know?

URSULA. I think you should tell me.

Pause.

VINCENT. When I came in just now, you had your head in your hands. I knew you were feeling bad. Then you denied it. Now tell me, which of us was telling the truth?

Pause.

URSULA. I got the tram back from the station, and it stopped at the ponds. There were crowds of people milling about in the sunlight. Boys and girls, all eyeing each other. One young man came out of the pub with so many glasses of beer in his hands and up his arms that he looked like an acrobat. Everyone clapped and cheered, and I can honestly say that I felt more wretched than I've felt in months. All I could see was youth and Spring and life renewing itself, and what for?

She laughs.

What for? It's futile, it's a mockery. That's why you found me as you did. Of course I wish you hadn't.

VINCENT. I have known for months. On the day I arrived, I was having a beer with Sam. He asked me, why were you dressed in black? I discovered the reason soon enough. It was in February. The snow was melting.

URSULA. Go on.

VINCENT. You had a black mood. That was his name for it. You wouldn't talk, or eat, or look at us. One day you shouted at

Eugenie. She was angry. I was the only one who understood. You'd fallen into the darkness of your soul. Have I offended you?

URSULA. No.

VINCENT. One night, I came downstairs at one in the morning and saw a light under your door. Then again at two, then again at three. I slept for a while, then something woke me. I came downstairs and as I got to the landing, I saw a white shape moving below me. It was you in your nightdress. I tiptoed back to my room, I looked out and I saw you sitting on the step of the garden shed. Like this.

He indicates, his head in his hands.

You looked up. I didn't move. We were like statues. Did you see me?

URSULA. No.

VINCENT. All that week, I woke at the quietest sound. The click of your door, the creak of a stair. I watched you. I watched *over* you. One day there was a bandage on your wrist. I hid the carving-knife. I hid the disinfectant. I went to the medicine chest, and hid the morphine and the laudanum. Did you not know it was me?

URSULA. No. I'd no idea. What on earth were you playing at?

VINCENT. I was protecting you.

URSULA. Oh for God's sake.

She gets up. Reaches for her exercise-books. He puts them further away. She reaches for them and he moves them again.

VINCENT. Where are you going?

URSULA. I can't stay here. Hand me those.

VINCENT. Not till you tell me . . .

URSULA (*loudly*). I was no risk to myself at all, none whatsoever. Now give me those books!

VINCENT. Here.

He gives her the books. She stands with them in her arms.

You knew it was me. Admit it.

She nods.

You see! We have a mental affinity! But I still don't know what made you so unhappy.

URSULA. Neither do I.

VINCENT. There must have been something.

URSULA. Yes, I'm sure there was.

VINCENT. What was it?

URSULA. I don't remember.

VINCENT. How could you not . . . ?

URSULA (*interrupts*). It was probably something unimportant. That's what it's like. It starts with something small and then it becomes about everything. And it's the 'everything' that makes me feel as I do. I can't explain it any better. I know it's awful for everyone else.

She sits, drinks her tea.

The stupid thing is that if I were asked in a court of law to swear it was genuine, that I wasn't just putting it on, I'd have to refuse. Because it could be mere indulgence. Perhaps it is. Perhaps I'm just a self-pitying old baggage. I don't know. I don't. I haven't the faintest.

VINCENT. I know these feelings.

URSULA. Let me assure you, Mr. Vincent, that whatever you feel is utterly different.

VINCENT. Who can say? I know I've sat in this kitchen, unable to open my heart. That hurt me. And it hurts to feel my life is wasted. I try to write poems, but all I can do is copy out other people's. I thought, if Sam can draw, then why not me? But the results were shameful. There's only one thing that gives me hope. That's you. You're like a mirror of my unhappiness. When I've watched you, like a big white moth in the moonlight . . . when I look at your face . . . your hands . . .

He looks at her hands. They're still for a moment.

Your ring. Your wedding ring. Where is it?

She looks at her left hand. Glances at the kitchen sink.

URSULA. I must have taken it off for safety.

He goes to the sink, looks.

VINCENT. No, it's not here.

URSULA. It must be somewhere upstairs.

VINCENT. I'll get it.

He goes to the door.

URSULA. Eugenie has it.

Pause.

I said Eugenie has it.

VINCENT. I heard you. Why does she have it?

URSULA. I lent it to her.

VINCENT. No, I don't understand

URSULA. Mr. Vincent, is it possible that you are as naive as you seem?

VINCENT. Of course!

URSULA. Then let me explain. In order to register at a hotel as man and wife, it's necessary for the woman to wear a wedding ring. My daughter, it seems, had bought a sixpenny ring to take to Broadstairs. But she forgot to take it to the station. I noticed her distress, and guessed the reason and I lent her mine.

VINCENT. You said she was staying with your sister.

URSULA. That's what *she* said. The truth is that she's sharing a hotel room with somebody else, someone very well known to you.

VINCENT. Who?

URSULA. Sam.

VINCENT. No, Sam is in Rochester.

URSULA. He *went* to Rochester. It's only thirty miles to Broadstairs on his bicycle. If he . . .

Stops, starts to laugh.

VINCENT. Why are you laughing?

URSULA. I don't know. I'm very upset.

VINCENT. Eugenie and Sam are staying as man and wife?

URSULA. Yes.

VINCENT. No, this is incredible. I cannot believe I'm hearing this. Do you mean they're married?

URSULA. They're in love.

VINCENT. Since when?

URSULA. Last winter.

VINCENT. But I was *here* last winter.

URSULA. It began before you arrived.

VINCENT. But *when* I arrived. *Still* nobody told me.

URSULA. We thought we wouldn't reveal the situation till we knew you better. Then once we did, we thought we'd better not.

VINCENT. Why?

URSULA. Because it's obvious that you cannot keep a secret.

VINCENT. Why is it secret?

URSULA. I run a school for young children. If it were known that my daughter was sleeping under the same roof as a young man with whom she had an understanding, I would have no more pupils. It's as simple as that.

VINCENT. Sam could have moved out.

URSULA. He could, but he didn't.

VINCENT. They could get married.

URSULA. Don't be absurd.

She gets up, moves about impatiently.

Think what it would mean for Sam. He'd be trapped. He'd be a common-or-garden painter and decorator till the end of his days. He'd be Mr. Bloggs who comes to paint the bathroom ceiling. Sam's better than that.

VINCENT. What about her? What kind of joy does it bring to a girl, to . . . No, I can't say it.

URSULA. She understands.

VINCENT. And did you . . . ? Did you know that they were going to . . . be together?

URSULA. One can know these things and not. I wasn't certain about it till this afternoon.

VINCENT. That's why you're sad.

URSULA. Oh, no, there's no connection. If two young people love each other, and they've waited as they have done, it would be wrong, quite wrong of me to take a contrary view. I believe that very strongly, Mr. Vincent.

She goes to pour tea.

I know it's a shock for you. I'm sorry.

VINCENT. No, it's fine.

Pause.

The funny thing is that I'm not upset. I feel quite pleased in a way. This house, that I thought was an empty place, was filled with love. And if the world contains some people who don't approve of what it's led to . . . we needn't worry about them. We can do as we like, and say as we like. So thank you.

Pause.

URSULA. It's getting dark.

VINCENT. I left the spade outside.

Pause.

I'll clear the shed out for you, if you . . .

He stops.

Maybe not.

Pause.

URSULA. It was a new departure for me. Sitting outside, I mean.
I'd crouch on the step, hunched up, and . . . oh, so desperate.
As though a storm was raging inside my brain. It was bitterly
cold, but the air had a kind of bite to it. I liked that.

She rubs an arm.

I'd look at things around me, perfectly humdrum things, a
patch of snow, or a knot in a piece of wood. I'd stare and
stare, and every bit of it would have a meaning. Heaven
knows what. It's odd, looking back on it. The nights were
clear, not a hint of fog. I've never seen so many stars in
London. I'd look up and . . . what I saw was the way I felt.
The sky was so black that there seemed to be no end to it, but
it was dotted with these brilliant, blazing lights. It was the
blackness and the brightness, both so different in a way,
but . . . No, I can't describe it. Then I'd think of myself, so
run-of-the-mill, so dreary . . . No, don't interrupt. It's fifteen
years since I talked about any of this. I'd look at the sky and
think, if you're worthless, if you despise yourself, but you're
able to see the best, most beautiful things that the world can
offer, then you'll never get there yourself, how could you?
But you can point the way. In my school, there's always one
boy worthy of being brought on. Although he may not know
it. Sam had no idea, when he first came to live here, what he
was capable of. I think, for them, it's like those dreams . . .
You're sitting at home, and you suddenly see an unfamiliar
door. You tease it open, and there's a room you've never seen
before, full of furniture and dust-sheets. Quite wonderful,
really.

VINCENT. Is that why you let me stay?

URSULA. No, that was different. When you told me about my daughter, I thought you were mad. I thought that nobody falls in love like that. I was just on the point of throwing you out, when I turned and looked . . . I thought I'd never seen anyone quite so . . . raw and suffering, yes, but quite so ruthless. I couldn't resist it. That was the moment, I suppose. And now you really will have to leave.

VINCENT. Let me tell you something. For months and months I've thought about your daughter. Now I can't remember what she looks like. All I can see is you. Her hair in yours, her eyes in yours . . .

She moves away.

Where are you going?

URSULA. Mr. Vincent, have you any idea how old I am?

VINCENT. Listen.

He opens the Michelet. Searches, finds the passage, reads:

'I see her still, modest and serious, with her black silk dress scarcely enlivened by a simple ribbon'.

He glances at her.

'This woman has been in my mind for thirty years, so innocent, so honest, so intelligent, yet lacking the cunning to see through the stratagems of this world.' . . . '*Il n'y a point de vieille femme, tant qu'elle aime et est aimé*'. 'No woman is old, as long as she loves and is loved.' I love you. I love your age. I love your unhappiness. And now, God help me, have I courage enough to cross this room?

URSULA. Why don't we sit for a moment?

They sit at opposite ends of the table.

VINCENT. So now we love each other.

URSULA. Yes.

VINCENT. And you are smiling.

URSULA. I was thinking of Ginny and Sam. I feel like children do when they're left alone in the house.

VINCENT. I feel that too. Have you had lovers since your husband died?

URSULA. No.

VINCENT. Do you mind my asking?

URSULA. No.

VINCENT. I've never been with a woman.

URSULA. I didn't think you had.

VINCENT. Someone in Holborn took me back to her room, but the atmosphere was not very *sympatique*, so I paid her the money she asked and went away.

Pause.

Let me tell you a story while you're still in love with me. My mother had a son who died on the day he was born.

He approaches her slowly.

They buried him at the door of my father's church. I was born one year later to the day. I used to read his gravestone every Sunday. His name was the same as mine. 'Vincent van Gogh, died March 30th, 1852'. I'd stand and read until they pulled me in to hear my father preach the sermon. Then I'd think about the amazing fact that I'd been born, and buried, and born all over again. That God had given me all my second chances rolled into one. And I'd never again have any others. Do you see what I'm saying? For me, it's once or never. Let me kiss you.

He reaches her. They kiss.

Do you hear my heart? It's beating so loud that I think it must make you deaf. You are a saint. An angel. No, I don't care about that. You are more beautiful than she is. I never loved her.

URSULA. You did.

VINCENT. Oh, *once* I did. I thought . . . how can I say it? Half of me thought I was in love. Now half of me knows. Don't puzzle your head about it.

He has unbuttoned her dress. Stands back.

URSULA. What is it?

VINCENT. Let me look at you.

End of Act Two.

ACT THREE

Sunday morning. Summer. The kettle is on. ANNA *comes in with a bucket and mop. She's eighteen: small, busy. She is cleaning a room upstairs. She changes the water, rinses the mop.*

SAM *comes in. He's been out, and has a hat and a Sunday paper.*

SAM. Hello!

ANNA. Good morning. I am sorry, I did not hear the doorbell.

SAM. I let myself in. You must be Anna van . . . Gock?

ANNA (*corrects him*). *Van Gogh!* But yes, I am Vincent's sister. I'm happy to meet you. You are . . . ?

SAM. Plowman's the name, Sam Plowman.

ANNA. Won't you please sit down and make yourself comfortable, Mr. Plowman. Excuse me that I cannot shake hands.

He sits.

Are you a friend of Vincent's?

SAM. I am. Did you arrive this morning?

ANNA. We did. It was a beautiful trip from Harwich. I cannot believe how green the fields are, even in summer. It will be hot today, I think. My brother has promised to take me to Buckingham Palace. May I make you a cup of tea?

SAM. That'd do nicely, thanks. Two sugars.

ANNA. Tea. Now where does she keep the tea? I will find it.

She looks for the tea.

Madame Tussaud's will be a treat for me. It is strange my brother has never been there. Tea. Tea.

SAM. It's there on the left. With 'Tea' written on it.

ANNA. Thank you. One for each person and one for the pot.

She makes the tea.

Vincent will be coming down quite soon. He is moving into the room they've given him. It is called a 'box-room'? But there are no boxes in it, only a bed and a *kastje.*

Gestures.

SAM. Chest of drawers.

ANNA. That is right. I am sorry to say the floor up there is none too clean.

SAM. I think you'll find that no-one expected you till Wednesday.

ANNA. That was the plan. But then my brother received a tele-gram from Goupil and Company about some urgent business. It was a disappointment for our parents that we had to leave so early. Still, as they say, work comes first. Sugar.

SAM. There.

She finds it.

ANNA. It seems you know this kitchen's ins and outs, Mr. Plowman. Are you a frequent visitor?

SAM. I live here. I'm the other lodger.

ANNA *looks at him with renewed interest.*

ANNA. Are you then romantically connected with Miss Loyer?

SAM. No, not a bit of it!

He laughs.

Never crossed my mind.

ANNA *snorts in disbelief. Turns away, inspects the teacup, washes it irritably.*

Did you have a nice crossing?

Pause.

I'm only asking 'cause I . . .

ANNA. It was uneventful.

SAM. No storms? 'Cause it was ever so windy here.

She clatters the cup and saucer.

Hurricanes? Shipwrecks? Trouble at customs?

ANNA. Here is your tea. I have my work.

VINCENT *looks through the door but doesn't come in. He has a portfolio and is tanned, shaggy and unshaven.*

VINCENT. Hello, Sam.

SAM. Hello old pal. Pull up a chair.

VINCENT. No, I . . .

ANNA. Vincent, I will put the finishing touches to my room now. When it is done, I will clean up yours.

She goes, taking her mop and bucket, ignoring SAM.

SAM. You've got a very peculiar sister.

VINCENT. Why?

SAM. Well, first she sat me down as though she owned the place, and then she asked a downright personal question.

VINCENT. Ignore her. She's over-excited.

SAM. Well, if you say so. I think washing other people's floors is *fairly* peculiar. I'll tell you something else. She makes a rotten cup of tea. Do you want some?

VINCENT. Please.

SAM. I'll do it.

VINCENT *sits.* SAM *pours him tea.*

What was it like?

VINCENT. Terrible. You don't know how lucky you are, Sam, not to have any family.

SAM. I'd never thought of it quite like that.

VINCENT. Oh yes. The thing about parents is, they just won't leave you alone. I went for walks, I went to bed, I went wherever I could to get away from them, and then my mother started crying, and that was painful for me.

SAM *gives him the tea.*

Thank you.

SAM. I got in.

VINCENT. What?

SAM. I got into college. I got the scholarship.

VINCENT. Sam, that's wonderful.

He goes to embrace SAM.

SAM. Here, mind the tea.

VINCENT. Oh yes.

Drinks his tea.

What did they say?

SAM. Not much. There was five of them sitting behind a big oak table. Tiled floor, Faux-Gothic ceiling and some very interesting murals.

Drinks his tea.

The table's at the far end, so it's a queasy walk. They sat me down, that was nice. Passed my portfolio down the table. One of them thought it lacked imagination. Big fat bastard. The others were fine.

VINCENT *glances into the hall.*

What?

VINCENT. Nothing. So they accepted you? That's good.

SAM. It is in a way. I couldn't help feeling that they saw me as . . . You know. A deserving case.

VINCENT. You are one.

SAM. Yes.

They drink their tea.

VINCENT. How much money will you get?

SAM. Twenty pounds.

VINCENT. A year?

SAM. Yes, obviously.

VINCENT. I thought it was more than that.

SAM. Well no, it's not.

VINCENT. Still, you can probably pick up something extra in the holidays.

SAM. And after hours and at the weekends. I can do it. But I'd need to know that I was good enough.

VINCENT. Oh yes.

SAM. You see what I'm asking.

VINCENT. What does *she* think?

SAM. Ginny?

VINCENT. No, her mother.

SAM. She's all smiles. At least that's *something* I've achieved. I'm asking you.

VINCENT. Have faith in yourself. I have faith in you, Sam. I do.

SAM. Honest?

VINCENT. Yes.

SAM. Well, thanks.

He gets up.

Where's Ginny?

VINCENT. She's in the schoolroom. Don't go just yet. I want to show you what I did in Holland.

He opens his portfolio. Of the first drawing to appear:

This was in The Hague. I'd gone to meet my brother, but he was stuck in a meeting so I had to wait. That's the parliament building across the lake. I tried to give the passers-by a kind of Japanese look.

SAM. Spiky.

VINCENT. Yes, they're too caricatured perhaps.

Next drawing.

This is a canal. It's in the countryside. I did the sky all over with a soft pencil and then I sort of painted it with the india rubber.

SAM. What are the birds for?

VINCENT. They were there.

SAM. Not all the time. Not stuck in the sky.

VINCENT. I wanted to show that it was evening.

Pause.

Let's try another one.

Turns over drawings.

Not that. Not that.

Next drawing.

This is the one I like. It's also evening. That's a kind of ditch we have at the side of a field to drain the water away.

SAM. A bird on a post.

VINCENT. Don't worry about the birds. I'd been reading a book about perspective. Thinking, oh, who cares about ridiculous old-fashioned nonsense? Then I saw this line of trees, so I thought I'd follow the rules for once, and guess what happened? It worked!

He laughs.

That's my father's church in the distance. There's his house.

SAM. I'm looking.

EUGENIE *comes in to make breakfast.*

EUGENIE. What's that?

SAM. Vincent's showing me his portfolio.

VINCENT. A portfolio is what you've got. This is sketches.

SAM is looking further down the portfolio. VINCENT *intercepts him.*

Don't look at those.

SAM turns back to the ditch drawing.

EUGENIE (*to* SAM). Do you want some breakfast?

SAM. I think I'll take my paper into the garden.

EUGENIE. Shall I bring you something out?

SAM. Yes, that'd be nice. Toast and tea and a couple of eggs. Will you come and sit with me?

EUGENIE. Yes, if you like.

SAM stops looking, closes the portfolio.

SAM. The sun's come out.

He gives the portfolio back to VINCENT. *Goes.* EUGENIE *puts bread against the fire. In time she will put eggs in boiling water, fill the kettle for tea, turn the toast.* VINCENT *watches SAM through the doorway.*

VINCENT. Sam's got everything now. A place at college. A fiancée. And not just any fiancée. You.

He turns to look at her.

You're looking different.

EUGENIE. How?

VINCENT. More peaceful.

EUGENIE. I'm not feeling very peaceful.

VINCENT. Why's that?

EUGENIE. Oh, things. I wish you'd keep your sister on a shorter lead.

VINCENT. Why, what do you mean?

EUGENIE. Well it was rather horrid. I was brushing my hair this morning, and I saw a shape in the mirror, so I jumped and turned around, and she was standing in the doorway.

VINCENT. What did you say to her?

EUGENIE. I didn't say anything. There wasn't time. She squeaked and ran up the stairs.

VINCENT. She must have mistaken the room.

EUGENIE. No, I don't think so. She'd taken her shoes off. She was holding them in her hand. She was poking around.

ANNA comes in with the mop and bucket.

ANNA. Excuse me please! I won't disturb your very private conversation. I am only to wash the *zwabber*.

EUGENIE. I'm going anyway.

She goes. ANNA runs water and rinses the mop in the bucket.

ANNA. Vincent, I must clean your floor. Go to your room and put your baggage on the bed.

VINCENT. *Zo meteen!*

ANNA. *Engels, alsjeblieft!* I need the practice. I am afraid that Mrs. Loyer's domestic staff is playing fast and loose with her. Later today I will take down all those cups and wash them.

VINCENT. Don't. Please don't. Just leave them. This is how people live in England. I know it's funny for us. They don't look after their houses like we do. You have to get used to it.

ANNA. *Now* you can talk! Now you are here in Brixton you can open your mouth! Why didn't you talk at home?

URSULA comes in dressed for the summer, not in black.

URSULA. You must be Anna!

ANNA. I'm happy to meet you, Mrs. Loyer.

URSULA. My dear, you shouldn't be doing that. Wouldn't you like some breakfast?

ANNA. We are not hungry, thank you. We ate on the train.

URSULA. Oh, in the dining-car? How very grand.

ANNA. We ate the food we brought from Holland. The dining-car is not for the likes of us. We must save our *dubbeltjies*.

She goes, taking a duster and clearing away SAM*'s hat en route.*

URSULA. Will she be doing this all the time?

VINCENT. It's what she's like.

They glance around. Move together, touch, then move a little way apart.

It will be easier when she's out all day.

URSULA. When will that be?

VINCENT. She has an interview on Thursday. Then another next week. It will be hard for her. People expect a governess to speak German.

URSULA. I would have thought her English was the problem. What are 'dubbeltjies'?

VINCENT. Small sums of money. Don't make fun of her.

They touch. There's a noise outside and they move apart. URSULA *covers by opening* VINCENT*'s portfolio.* EUGENIE *comes in with a tray. She makes tea, assembles breakfast. Meanwhile:*

VINCENT. I told Eugenie that she's looking different.

URSULA. I've not noticed.

VINCENT. Maybe because you see her every day.

EUGENIE. He's looking *very* different, isn't he, mother? With his face all brown and his hair like that. He looks like Baby Bear. He ought to be eating porridge.

URSULA. He should eat something.

EUGENIE. I can do you an egg. Have one of Sam's.

VINCENT. I'm not hungry.

EUGENIE. Mother?

URSULA. No, thank you, darling.

EUGENIE *takes* SAM's *breakfast out into the garden.*
URSULA *is still looking at* VINCENT's *portfolio.*

VINCENT. Don't *glance* at that.

URSULA. I wasn't.

VINCENT. Give it to me.

He takes the portfolio. Sits or moves away, protecting it with his arms.

My sister told me . . . now it is me who is making fun . . .
that I should put my baggage on my bed. I wanted to laugh,
because I thought that, when the house is empty, that is what
I will do with you.

URSULA. But it isn't just that.

VINCENT. No, it's other things too. It's books and
conversations and the fact that my drawing is so much better.
But it *is* just that, and the other things follow. When I was at
home, I thought about it all the time. I wanted to see you
naked, like you were when I drew you.

He opens his portfolio, finds the drawing.

Lying on your side, your flesh hanging loose, looking up so
boldly, though I could only get you to do that for half a
minute. And underneath I wrote the truest words I know.
'No woman is old, as long as she loves and is loved.'

He closes the portfolio.

At home, they asked me, 'Why don't you talk to us? Why
aren't you telling our visitors what it's like in London?' But
the only thing worth saying was what I couldn't tell them.
I went for a walk on Sunday evening. I stopped and looked
at my father's church across the fields. The bells were ringing

for the service that I should have gone to. It was the sight and the sound which had pulled me away from you. I thought my heart would break with missing you. And then I thought, God damn, what kind of cowardly bastard am I, to feel so strongly and not do anything with it? So I drew. And that was my first landscape that isn't too bad.

He opens the portfolio and shows her. ANNA comes in with her duster.

ANNA. Vincent, will you do as I said?

VINCENT *closes the portfolio and goes, leaving it on the table. ANNA gets the mop out of the bucket and squeezes it dry. Meanwhile:*

My brother is quite a handful, Mrs. Loyer. You should hear my father. 'Where is that *'pummel'*?' 'Why is that *'pummel'* still in bed?' I must explain. A *'pummel'* in Dutch is what you would call . . .

URSULA. I'm sure I know what it means.

ANNA. My first present to you will be a pretty oilcloth to put over this table. We shall have many pleasant talks around it. But Mr. Plowman must not be sly with me. I was quite cold with him this morning.

URSULA. I beg your pardon?

ANNA. I know all about his feeling for your daughter. In Holland it would not be *comme il faut* that he is living here. That is not my business.

URSULA. No, it isn't.

ANNA. But I worry that it will give my brother nervous strain.

URSULA. Why should it?

ANNA. Because it's hard for Vincent to conceal his feelings.

URSULA. I doubt there's anything to conceal. Your brother and Mr. Plowman are very good friends. And they have many things in common.

ANNA *laughs.*

ANNA. *Too* many perhaps?

URSULA. What are you talking about?

ANNA. Is it not true that *both* these young men are in love with your daughter?

URSULA. No, certainly not! Wherever did you pick up that idea?

ANNA. I am thinking now of the letter that Vincent wrote me when he first moved in.

She has brought the letter down with her.

We were worried, because we did not know if this was quite a respectable area.

She opens the letter, reads.

I will translate. First he describes her . . . so and so and so, 'a girl of whom I have agreed we should be brother and sister.'

URSULA. Well?

ANNA. 'You . . . ' that's me, ' . . . should also consider her a sister . . . ' And then, 'You must not think that there is more to this than I have written.'

URSULA. That's it?

ANNA. That's it.

URSULA. Then I don't see what the fuss is about.

ANNA. My feeling was, and my sisters agreed, that there was more than a brother-and-sisterly feeling here. I felt there would grow a love between my brother and your daughter such as between David Copperfield and Agnes.

URSULA. David Copperfield and Agnes *are* like brother and sister.

ANNA. But they get married in the end.

URSULA. That's an absurd comparison.

ANNA. Come, Mrs. Loyer. When you heard this letter, did it not hint at something deeper?

URSULA. One could read an emotion into it, yes.

ANNA. And did that emotion not exist?

URSULA. Since you ask . . . on the day he arrived . . . he might have felt a certain attraction. We talked about it and he put it aside, and now it's over and done with.

ANNA. Are you certain of that?

URSULA. I know it.

ANNA. Forgive me for persisting. Is he then in love with some equally young and attractive woman?

URSULA. I can truthfully say he isn't.

ANNA. Good. That's good. Then nobody's heart will be broken when he is transferred to Paris.

URSULA. What did you say?

ANNA. Did you not know? It is all arranged.

EUGENIE *comes in from the garden.*

EUGENIE. It's lovely outside. Why don't you join us?

URSULA. Have you heard the news?

EUGENIE. No, what?

URSULA. Vincent's being transferred to Paris.

EUGENIE. When?

URSULA. I don't know. I've only just heard.

ANNA. He will go when I have found a job as governess.

EUGENIE. He's a beast for not telling us.

URSULA. Though we knew it was bound to happen.

EUGENIE (*to* ANNA). Does this mean he's been promoted?

ANNA *laughs.*

ANNA. No, I don't think promotion is very likely. It will be good experience for him. There are more good painters there than there are in England. Also certain new ones who are terrible rubbish, but my brother won't have to deal with those.

EUGENIE. I'll miss him.

URSULA. We all will.

Sharply to ANNA, *who is picking up her mop and bucket:*

Leave that please.

ANNA. What?

URSULA. You've been clattering round since seven o'clock. I'm getting a headache.

EUGENIE. Mother.

ANNA. I was only . . .

EUGENIE. Ssh.

URSULA. I think a walk might do me good. Eugenie darling, if I'm not back for a while, will you start preparing dinner? Thank you for telling us, Anna.

She goes. EUGENIE *starts washing up.*

ANNA. I think I asked too many questions.

EUGENIE. Very likely.

ANNA. I have a lot to learn in London. Later this week you must show me how to do my hair. Though mine is thicker than yours. I like your dress.

EUGENIE. Thank you.

ANNA *looks at her for a moment, then looks away.*

ANNA. It's funny, you know . . . how if one comes from a different country . . . and if one is young . . . then people think one is naive.

EUGENIE. I find you anything but naive. If that's any comfort to you.

ANNA. People forget, that in the house of a country pastor, one hears more of sin and error than in many a city. Think the worst, and it's probably true. That's my experience.

EUGENIE. How very depressing.

ANNA. My brother is good at heart, but he's easily led. We hoped that in London he would develop a stronger character. For a while, I think he did. But then we heard quite recently that . . .

EUGENIE. I don't know why you're telling me this.

ANNA. It is to do with you. We heard that he was late for work, that he was taking off days to be sick. That's why my father brought him home. But we were shocked to see him. He drank, he smoked a pipe, he took the name of the Lord in vain. We could accept all this. There's a black sheep in every family. What made us so upset was how unhappy he was. He wouldn't talk. He left the house all day. He cut himself off from the people who love him. We knew there must be a woman to blame. I asked him, was it you?

EUGENIE. This is ridiculous.

ANNA. I pressed him hard, and he admitted at last the lodger was your suitor. That was true. But why did he want to return to London three days early? He said he had a telegram. There was no telegram. I asked the postmistress.

EUGENIE. This is utterly mad.

ANNA. Why would he lie, unless you were still entangling him? There is no other woman. I asked your mother. He wanted you from the day he arrived . . .

EUGENIE. What rubbish.

ANNA. It's true. Your mother told me. But then she lied, and said that . . .

EUGENIE. How dare you say that?

ANNA. I'm sorry.

EUGENIE. So you should be. I've never heard such nonsense. It's outrageous.

ANNA. What do you think it's like for me? I didn't even want to come to London.

SAM comes in from the garden.

SAM. What's happening?

EUGENIE. We're going out.

SAM. Where?

EUGENIE. It doesn't matter. Get your hat.

He goes out. To ANNA*:*

While you're here, which I hope won't be for very much longer, I must ask you to keep your filthy suspicions to yourself. And stay out of my bedroom.

ANNA. I will. I'm sorry you saw me. But how can I know what secrets are in this house unless I look for them?

EUGENIE. There *are* no secrets.

ANNA. There are. I know there are.

She reaches out in a desperate appeal.

Oh, let him go! Let him go! I beg you! He's been a failure all his life. Nobody in the family thinks he will come to anything. Must we do nothing to save him? From a woman who keeps two men on her arm? Who loves one of them one day, and the other the next?

She looks pointedly at ANNA*'s stomach.*

Of the nature of that love, I say nothing. You know what I mean.

SAM looks in.

EUGENIE. It's all right, Sammy. Wait on the pavement.

SAM. I will. I'll do that.

He goes.

EUGENIE. What I don't understand is how a decent man like Vincent could have such a disgusting family.

ANNA. We're not. We're good. It's you who are wicked.

EUGENIE. As for you, you're obviously very stupid. If he'd
really told my mother . . . what you say . . . that he'd some
interest in me . . . do you honestly think for a minute that
she'd have let him move in? Well?

She goes. ANNA *sits, baffled and upset. The front door opens
and closes:* SAM *and* EUGENIE *have gone out.*

ANNA *notices* VINCENT*'s portfolio. She opens it and finds
a drawing of Dutch landscape. She looks at it with nostalgia
and puts it out on the table. Takes out a few more, arranges
them in a pleasing sequence. Continues, then suddenly stops:
she's found the nude drawing of* URSULA.

VINCENT *comes in, sees her.* ANNA *reads to him,
translating as she goes:*

ANNA. 'No woman is old, as long as she loves and is loved.'
So it was her.

VINCENT. Yes.

ANNA. Why didn't you tell her you were going to Paris?

VINCENT. Because I'm staying in London.

ANNA. I think that when our father wants a thing to happen,
then it happens. I will say nothing to him. Nor to our mother,
nor to anyone else. But we must leave this house today, and
never come back.

VINCENT. I'm not leaving.

ANNA. Well, you must choose your path. I was horrible to the
daughter. I am sorry now. I was so worried to think you were
the father of her child.

VINCENT. What?

ANNA. Did you not know that she is pregnant?

VINCENT. No.

ANNA. Did your friend Mr. Plowman not tell you?

VINCENT. No.

ANNA. Nor her mother?

VINCENT. I'm sure she hasn't noticed.

ANNA. Vincent, if you knew how much your family loves you, you would not have chosen this one.

VINCENT. You don't understand.

ANNA. I am glad I don't. What I must do, for now, is pack my bags. I have all day to find new lodgings. You may come if you change your mind. I hope you will.

She goes out. VINCENT *looks at the drawing. Closes the portfolio so that it looks as it did before.* URSULA *comes in, fills the kettle.*

URSULA. Where's your sister?

VINCENT. She's gone upstairs.

URSULA. I hear you're being transferred.

VINCENT. No, nothing's fixed.

URSULA. That's not what Anna says.

VINCENT. It's what my father wants, that's all. He told my uncle and my uncle told the manager. The truth is, nobody at Goupil cares *where* I go.

URSULA. Well don't feel bound by me.

VINCENT. I won't.

URSULA. You do what you like. You needn't explain, you needn't apologise. I want it clean and swift and sharp. That's how I want it.

VINCENT. You want whatever will make you most unhappy. Ask it from anyone else, but not from me.

There is a noise on the stairs: ANNA *is moving a suitcase.*

URSULA. *Now* what's she doing?

VINCENT. I don't know. What did you think about my drawings?

URSULA. Well, as you said, I only glanced at them.

VINCENT. No, that was foolish of me. I did them for you, so I was frightened of what you'd think.

URSULA. They're good.

VINCENT. How good?

URSULA. I liked the one with the church. At least I did when I saw it at first.

VINCENT. And then?

She looks at him, makes a choice.

URSULA. Then you told about the way you'd felt that day . . . all that fury, all that anger and confusion . . . and I looked at the drawing again and I couldn't see any of that. That was the most important thing that was happening at that moment, and you left it out.

VINCENT. I see. Well, thank you.

URSULA *goes out. Shortly after,* ANNA *appears at the door.*

ANNA (*whispers*). She's in her room. I must go this minute. What will you do?

VINCENT. I don't know.

End of Act Three.

ACT FOUR

Autumn. Evening. Thunder. It's raining outside. URSULA *comes in with a lamp. She wears her old black dress. At some point she sits, hunched up, perhaps with her head in her hands.*

EUGENIE *comes in. She's come from outside, and is carrying a baby.*

EUGENIE. I nipped my finger getting the pram up the steps.

She sucks her finger.

It's freezing in the hall. I don't know how you put up with it. Do you want some tea?

No answer.

I know I do. Will you hold her for me? Just for a minute while I put the kettle on?

No answer.

I'll fetch the pram in.

She goes out. URSULA *stays seated.* EUGENIE *comes back wheeling the pram with the baby in it. She places it in a corner and puts the kettle on.*

The fire's going nicely. Has Sammy been round?

She sees a newspaper on the table.

Yes, there's his paper. He tells me nothing, that boy.

She starts laying out teacups.

Why didn't he stay? He knew I was coming to see you.

URSULA *looks for something, finds a note. Holds it out to* EUGENIE.

What?

She takes the note and reads it.

'Gone home to get my . . . '

Pause.

Mother?

Pause.

What does Sammy want his toolbag for?

URSULA *replies in a flat voice, inaudible.*

URSULA. Skirting-board.

EUGENIE. Oh mother, speak up!

URSULA (*aggressive*). He's fixing a skirting-board upstairs.

EUGENIE. Oh. Oh well that's nice of him.

URSULA. I didn't ask him to.

EUGENIE. I'm sure you didn't.

URSULA. I don't know why he left a note. I suppose he thought I wasn't competent to tell you myself.

EUGENIE. He wasn't being nasty, mother. You do forget things.

Thunder.

He'll get soaked.

There are exercise-books on the table. She opens one.

I'll take these home if you like. I'll mark them tonight and Sammy can pop them round in the morning.

The baby whimpers. EUGENIE *starts getting ready to feed her. The doorbell rings.*

He's forgotten his key.

She goes out. Muffled voices are heard from the front door. URSULA *stays seated.* EUGENIE *comes back.*

Mother.

No answer.

Mother, it's Mr. Vincent.

Pause.

He's out on the doorstep. He wants to know if you'll let him
in.

Pause.

That's what he said. What do you want me to do? It's raining.

No answer. She goes out. After a few moments she shows
VINCENT *into the room. He's wild-looking and dripping wet*
from the rain and his clothes are old and worn-through. He
sees URSULA.

(*Unfriendly.*) I'll have to leave you with her, I'm afraid. You'd
better take that coat off.

VINCENT. Thank you.

He takes off his coat. EUGENIE *hangs it on the clothes-*
horse in front of the fire.

EUGENIE. I'll make some tea when I come back down.

VINCENT. Have you got anything to eat?

EUGENIE. There's some cake from yesterday. It's in the tin,
you can help yourself.

He opens the tin, finds the remains of a home-made cake with
candles on it. EUGENIE *lifts the baby out of the pram.*

VINCENT. You had the baby.

EUGENIE. Mm hm.

VINCENT. Is it a boy or a girl?

EUGENIE. This is a girl. The first was a boy. He's two-and-a-
bit. You need a calendar.

She takes the baby out to feed it. VINCENT *eats some cake.*
After a few moments:

VINCENT. Brixton has changed. Everywhere I walked, I saw
the faces of the poor. I find them beautiful now. Some ragged

boys had built a bonfire near the ponds. But then the rain came down.

Pause.

She said I mustn't stay long.

URSULA. No word, no explanation. Not even a note.

VINCENT. It's what seemed best.

URSULA. There are some things of yours in the box-room. Books, letters, I don't know what, I haven't seen them. Sam can sort them out for you. I suppose that's what you came for.

VINCENT. I came for this.

He indicates the cake he's eating.

It was your birthday yesterday. I brought you these.

He takes a bunch of violets out of his pocket.

London violets. The woman who sold them to me said they bloom twice a year. First in the Spring, and now in Autumn. Shall I put them in water for you?

URSULA. I'll do it.

She stands, takes the flowers, fills a little vase and puts them in it.

VINCENT. Two little children. Are they like him or her?

URSULA. I couldn't say. They're not distinctive. They're just ordinary babies. Take off those boots. Go on.

VINCENT *unties his sodden, battered old boots.* SAM *enters, wet from the rain, carrying his toolbag. He doesn't immediately recognise* VINCENT, *but sees the pram.*

SAM. It's pelting down out there. Where's Ginny got to?

VINCENT. Hello, Sam.

SAM. Blimey. This is a turn-up. What happened to you?

VINCENT. I was caught in the rain.

SAM. Oh, raining, is it? That explains it.

He laughs.

No, what I *meant* was . . .

URSULA. Eugenie's upstairs.

SAM. Oh, fine. (*To* VINCENT.) Are you stopping or going?

URSULA. He'll stay for a cup of tea.

SAM. I'll see you. (*Of* VINCENT*'s boots.*) You can use my paper for those. Leave me the racing pages.

He goes. VINCENT *looks at the newspaper, unsure of what to do with it.* URSULA *makes tea.*

URSULA. Did you really go to Paris?

VINCENT. Yes of course. I don't know why you ask me in that sceptical way.

URSULA. You don't look like a Parisian art dealer.

VINCENT. I lost my job. It was the customers' fault. They were always wanting to buy the wrong paintings and there was nothing I could do or say to stop them. 'Against stupidity the Gods thunder in vain.' So there I was. At twenty-two, a redundant person. Then, with God's good help, I was offered a job in England. At a school. Do you still have your school?

URSULA. I do. It's smaller now, I'm not very much involved. Bridget helps. Bridget the maid. She's good with children. Give me those.

She takes the boots, tears paper from the newspaper and stuffs it into them.

VINCENT. I'm teaching now in a place called Isleworth. It's just past Richmond. The school is run by a very fine man, a minister of the Congregational Church. I like the place. If you could see the empty playground in the evening, with the river behind it. In the house, the gas is flickering, and I hear the sound of the boys at homework. One of them starts a hymn, and they all join in. 'Tell me the old, old story, of Jesus and

His love.' Then I think the Lord has taken me to his heart,
with all my faults.

URSULA. Have you been drawing?

VINCENT. No.

She turns away, pours tea for them both.

What about Sam, did he go to college?

URSULA. No.

VINCENT. Why not?

URSULA. He couldn't afford it.

VINCENT *laughs quietly to himself.*

What's the joke?

VINCENT. *He* couldn't afford it. That's so funny. Look at my
overcoat. Look at those boots.

URSULA. You can choose your life. Sam has a wife and family
to support.

VINCENT. Then he's a big fool. An artist doesn't care for his
wife or children, any more than for the pigeons in the park.
He cares for himself and for his work. If Sam can't see that,
he doesn't deserve to be an artist.

URSULA. How *dare* you patronise him? What have you done to
be so grand about? You've not done anything.

VINCENT. Would it make any difference to you if I had?

URSULA. You've not been drawing.

VINCENT. Only because I've found a better medium.

URSULA. Do you mean, you're painting?

VINCENT. No.

URSULA. Etching? Sculpting? What are you talking about?

VINCENT. When Jesus wrote, what did he write on?

URSULA. I've no idea.

VINCENT. The earth. The sand. John, chapter 8, verse 6. 'Jesus stooped down, and with his finger wrote on the ground, as though he heard them not.' If he had drawn, he would have done the same. Because the wind would blow it away, the tide would cover it. That's what he was teaching us. That's how he showed his contempt for paper and clay and canvas. Jesus didn't write books, he didn't paint pictures. Yet he was the greatest artist of all time. Greater than Rembrandt, greater than Michelangelo. Because he chose for his medium, flesh. The living man. I'll do the same. I will become a preacher. I will live with the poor, I will share their poverty and I will teach them the word of God. And then I'll truly be an artist.

URSULA *throws a plate at him.*

URSULA. Will you stop that?

Pause.

Don't tell them.

VINCENT. I won't.

URSULA. They hate me. They want to put me somewhere awful, I know it.

SAM *is heard coming downstairs.* VINCENT *starts picking up the broken plate.* SAM *comes in, carrying the old bit of skirting-board. He sees* VINCENT.

SAM. Hello.

VINCENT. I dropped a plate.

SAM. I heard it.

To URSULA:

SAM. I got the old bit out, and look at it. It's like a sponge. Good job I spotted it.

He puts it out the back door.

Tea's up I see. Ginny's dying for a cuppa.

URSULA. I'll take her one.

SAM. Only if you're up to it.

URSULA. I can manage.

She goes, taking a cup of tea. SAM *washes his hands.*

SAM. What do you think?

VINCENT. She will get better with God's help. I think she's
frightened that . . . I don't know how to say this. That you'll
put her somewhere that she can't get away from. That's what
she's afraid of.

SAM. I can't think why. I'm sure it's nothing *I've* said.

Uncomfortable pause.

Ginny don't mean half of what she comes out with. She gets
upset, that's all. She comes round here with food and library
books, and never a word of welcome. Just a thick black fog
in every corner. It's not very nice, with the kids and all. The
school's gone hang, did Ma not tell you?

VINCENT. She says that Bridget's doing the teaching.

SAM. None of those boys will go to the Grammar. It all started
up again when you left.

VINCENT. Oh yes?

SAM. She took to her bed. Drew the curtains, wouldn't come
out. Then when she did, it was as though all her small moods
had joined up into one big one. Like she'd given up hope.

VINCENT. I see.

Pause.

What are you looking at?

SAM. I promised myself that if I ever saw you again, I'd ask
you something.

VINCENT. Well?

SAM. Is it true?

VINCENT. Is what true?

SAM. Is it true what I'm thinking?

VINCENT. You can think what you like. But it's none of your business.

SAM. I think I've got my answer. With her?

VINCENT. Yes.

SAM. Really?

VINCENT. Yes.

SAM. I've got to sit down for a minute. Are you having me on?

VINCENT. No.

SAM. Well bugger me.

VINCENT. How did you know?

SAM. I didn't. The jigsaw sort of shuffled itself about and . . . I didn't believe it, though, till . . . Was it . . . ? You know. Was it . . . *properly*?

VINCENT. Yes. Oh yes. Does Eugenie know?

SAM. She won't let on. I've tried bringing it up, but she just changes the subject.

VINCENT. What about you, are you disgusted?

SAM. I don't know. I'm sure I *should* be.

Thinks.

No, not really. I feel sad, that's all. I can't help thinking that if that's what you and the old girl wanted . . . sorry . . .

VINCENT. No, go on.

SAM. . . . then you shouldn't have run away. In the way you did. It was a cowardly act.

VINCENT. We all of us run away from something.

SAM. No we don't.

VINCENT. You were going to be an artist. Then the baby happened. And you ran as far as your legs would take you.

SAM. Bollocks.

He laughs.

I *could* have run. Don't think I didn't consider it. San Francisco seemed attractive for a couple of days. The Foreign Legion. North London. And I considered the artist's life as well, but I decided not to bother.

VINCENT. No, that's not true. I remember it clearly. You were excited. You were only worried about the money. Then I showed you what I had done myself. And . . .

SAM. That's when I decided.

VINCENT. No. Don't try to make me feel bad, Sam. That's an underhand trick. Those drawings of mine were mediocre.

SAM. If you say so. I just thought I'd quit before you did any good ones.

URSULA *comes in. To her:*

All right, ma? Have your tea.

He goes to the door.

There's people round here, you know, who'd slap a couple of coats of paint on that old skirting-board. Then you'd wonder why the plaster had blown.

To VINCENT:

It worked out fine, by the way. Just thought I'd tell you.

He goes.

URSULA. Was he talking about me?

VINCENT. He says you've given up hope.

URSULA. That's not mad. It's just a practical view of the way things are.

VINCENT. You would say that.

URSULA. All I wanted was .. some day, somehow . . . to be the cause of something remarkable. Not in myself, of course. I'm not a talented woman. I'm rather dull, in most of the ways that matter. But I am sincere. And my desire, my longing for somebody near to me to get out of the rut, to reach for something higher than *this*, was real. Was genuine. That's why I started the school. Then there was Sam. Dear, kind man that he is. It was wrong of me to push him. And I had hopes of you. But what's happened is so unbelievably foolish, so disgraceful, that I can't even look at you now. It's like a terrible joke. As though my great ideal could only take shape in a ludicrous form. In the form of someone I loved, who became the next best thing to a tramp and rambled on and on about Jesus. It appals me. I've heard more sense from lunatics on street corners.

She cries silently.

VINCENT. The road is hard. But Christ is there for us at the end.

URSULA. Please stop.

VINCENT. There was a man called Nicodemus. He went to our Lord, and asked him, 'What must I do to be saved?' . . .

URSULA. I mean it.

VINCENT. Jesus answered, 'Sell all your goods and give the money to the poor.' Which Nicodemus wasn't expecting.

He laughs.

Such was his luck, he had a question, and there was Jesus himself to give him the answer, but it wasn't the one he wanted. So he went away – and this is the beautiful word that it says in your English Bible – 'sorrowful'. That's how I left this house. I don't know why I went. My sister said it was time to go. I could have stayed, but the moment passed. It was as though my baby brother, my dead self, had reached his arm from the grave and pulled me down into his world of sighs and tears. Ever since then, I've lived in sorrow. This is your gift to me. It never leaves me now. It's black and it's bright, just like you said. It's like stars in the sky.

SAM *and* EUGENIE *are heard coming down the stairs.*

They're coming down.

SAM and EUGENIE *come in.* SAM *has his toolbag.*
EUGENIE *puts the baby in the pram.*

SAM. That'll do for now. I'll look at it during the week.

EUGENIE. We ought to go. Little Sammy will be waiting.

SAM. I never had no tea.

EUGENIE. 'Never 'ad no tea'. The way he talks now. Shall
I make a new pot?

SAM. I *like* it strong (*i.e., don't bother*).

EUGENIE *about to pour his tea, sees* VINCENT'*s boots on
a sheet of newspaper on the table.*

EUGENIE. Oh mother!

SAM. Move them, then.

He finds her a chair.

Go on, sit down.

VINCENT *looks at the boots.* URSULA *watches him. The
baby whimpers:* EUGENIE *picks her out of the pram.*

EUGENIE (*to the baby*). Who's that? Mm? It's Mr. Vincent.
He's a Dutchman.

SAM *tries to get* URSULA'*s attention:*

SAM. Here, ma.

EUGENIE. Don't bother her, Sam, she's thinking.

SAM. No she's not. She's listening. Aren't you, ma? Ginny said
last night that her nanna could tell fortunes.

URSULA. Well . . . so she claimed.

She turns her gaze back to VINCENT, *as he picks up an
exercise-book and pencil.*

SAM (*to* EUGENIE). What did I say?

EUGENIE. She *did* tell fortunes. She used to make me swizzle
my teacup round and put it upside-down on the saucer. Then

she'd pick it up, and look inside and see a zebra, or a bowler hat, or whatever it was.

SAM. Who'll finish the cake? (*To* VINCENT.) We had a party yesterday.

VINCENT *nods, not really listening. Looks at the boots.*

EUGENIE. Just a small one. Sammy and mother and me and the children.

SAM. It was nice.

EUGENIE. The cake was nice.

SAM (*of* VINCENT). Good job *he* wasn't here to count the candles.

EUGENIE (*with unexpected vehemence*). Shut up, Sammy!

SAM. What is it now? All I said was . . .

EUGENIE. We heard you.

SAM *hums a tune, reads what's left of the paper.* EUGENIE *jiggles the baby.*

Unnoticed by SAM *and* EUGENIE, VINCENT *starts drawing the boots.* URSULA *watches.*

End of play.